The KDP Playbook

A No-Nonsense Guide to Building & Scaling a Profitable Self-Publishing Business

An Online Income Playbook

CONTENTS

Introduction: Embracing the Journey of Self-
Publishing   v

1. Developing the Right Mindset for Publishing
Success   1
2. Finding the Right Topic & Market Research   7
3. Outlining Your Book   18
4. Writing Your First Kindle Book   24
5. Helping Others Publish – Turning Book Creation
Into a Business   32
6. Formatting and Preparing Your Book for Kindle
Publishing   39
7. Designing a Professional Book Cover   46
8. Publishing Your Book on KDP   52
9. Pricing & Royalties – How to Maximize Profit   59
10. Marketing & Generating Sales   66
11. Scaling Your Publishing Business   74
12. Overcoming Challenges & Avoiding Common
Pitfalls   82
13. Long-Term Strategies & Building a Sustainable
Publishing Business   89
14. Conclusion – Your Publishing Journey   96

Introduction: Embracing the Journey of Self-Publishing

Welcome to the World of Kindle Direct Publishing (KDP)

In 2011, an unknown author named **Hugh Howey** self-published a short story on Amazon called *Wool*. Readers loved it, and within months, demand skyrocketed. He expanded it into a novel, and by 2012, he was making **six figures a month** in royalties. Eventually, he signed a **print-only** deal with a major publisher while keeping the digital rights—and full control—of his work.

His story isn't unique. Thousands of independent authors are making a living through self-publishing—**without relying on traditional publishers.**

Publishing used to be an exclusive club, where getting your book into readers' hands required agents, editors, and a stroke of luck. Today, the **game has changed**. With **Kindle Direct Publishing (KDP)**, you can publish your book, make it available worldwide, and start earning royalties—all **without** waiting for someone else's approval.

But before we dive into the details, take a moment to ask yourself:

- Why do you want to publish a book?
- Is it to share your story? Build a brand? Create an income stream?
- How can self-publishing fit into a **bigger, more sustainable vision** for your life?

The journey from **writer to published author** isn't just about finishing a book—it's about **embracing the mindset of an author-preneur** and building something meaningful that lasts.

THE POWER OF THOUGHTFUL PLANNING

Many new authors make the mistake of **rushing to publish** without a clear plan. The excitement of finishing a manuscript often leads to impulsive decisions—uploading too soon, skipping professional editing, or neglecting marketing.

The truth is, **great books aren't just written—they're crafted.**

Your ideas will evolve, and that's a **good** thing. The key is to:

- Take the time to **refine your vision.**
- **Outline and structure** your book strategically.
- Approach self-publishing as a **business**, not just a creative outlet.

Likewise, while **AI and writing tools** can help with brainstorming, they **can't replace** the human touch. The depth, nuance, and emotional connection in your writing must come from **you.**

Self-publishing isn't about **uploading and hoping**—it's about **building a creative business** that aligns with your long-term goals.

What to Expect in This Book

By the time you finish this book, you won't just know **how to publish**—you'll have a **blueprint for building a long-term publishing career.**

We'll walk through the **self-publishing journey step by step,** covering:

- **The Right Mindset for Success** – How to think like a self-published author and approach it as a business.
- **Writing & Developing Your Book** – Strategies for writing, outlining, and editing—whether you have funds to invest or not.
- **Formatting & Publishing Like a Pro** – Preparing your book for a professional release on KDP.
- **Marketing & Selling Your Book** – How to **attract readers, build an audience, and drive sales**—even if you're starting from scratch.
- **Scaling & Expanding Your Business** – Turning your writing into a sustainable income stream, including **audiobooks, translations, and expanding beyond Amazon.**

By the end, you won't just know **how to publish**—you'll understand **how to thrive as an independent author.**

A Word on Mindset and Perseverance

Self-publishing can feel overwhelming, and that's completely normal. The sheer amount of information out there can lead to **analysis paralysis.**

The secret? **Take it one step at a time.**

I've been where you are—excited, uncertain, and unsure of where to begin. But I've also seen **how self-publishing can transform lives.** It gives you control, **freedom,** and the ability to turn your passion into a **real career.**

This guide is here to **simplify the process**—whether you're publishing your first book or optimizing your approach.

What is KDP?

Kindle Direct Publishing (KDP) is **Amazon's self-publishing platform,** allowing authors to publish and sell eBooks and paperbacks worldwide. Since its launch in 2007, **KDP has revolutionized publishing,** removing traditional gatekeepers and giving authors full control over their work.

With KDP, you can:

- **Upload your book** and have it available for sale within **hours.**
- **Set your own price** and update it whenever you want.
- **Reach millions of readers** without paying upfront costs.

KDP isn't just a publishing platform—it's a **gateway to a global audience.**

Why Choose KDP?

Many authors start with KDP because it offers:

- **No upfront costs** – Publish without paying for inventory or distribution.
- **Global reach** – Your book is available across **multiple Amazon marketplaces.**

- **Full control** – Set your price, update your book anytime, and retain rights to your work.
- **Higher royalties** – Earn **up to 70% on eBooks**, far more than traditional publishers typically offer.

With **Amazon owning a significant share of the book market,** KDP is the **best place to start** before expanding your reach.

Later in this book, we'll explore strategies for **"going wide"**— publishing on multiple platforms to **maximize your earnings and audience.**

Traditional Publishing vs. KDP

Traditional publishing still exists, but it comes with **major hurdles:**

- **Finding a literary agent** – Most publishers won't consider unsolicited manuscripts.
- **Selective acceptance** – Even with an agent, publishers **reject most books.**
- **Loss of control** – Publishers decide your book's title, cover, pricing, and distribution.
- **Slow timeline** – It can take **years** to see your book in print.

KDP eliminates these roadblocks:

- **No gatekeepers** – Anyone can publish, regardless of background or connections.
- **Creative control** – You decide **everything**, from cover design to pricing.
- **Faster publishing timeline** – Upload today, **sell tomorrow.**

The trade-off? **You're responsible for marketing and sales—but that also means you keep more of your earnings.**

Is KDP Right for You?

Ask yourself:

- Do you want **creative control** over your book's content, pricing, and design?
- Are you **willing to learn** marketing, publishing, and audience-building strategies?
- Do you want **global reach** without relying on traditional publishers?
- Are you comfortable taking **full responsibility** for your book's success?

If you answered **yes** to most of these, **KDP is a great place to start.**

The Future of Publishing

The **publishing industry is shifting**. While traditional publishing still has a place, **self-publishing has leveled the playing field**. You no longer need a publisher to reach readers—you can **do it yourself.**

But there's one key difference between authors who **succeed** and those who **struggle...**

It's not talent. It's **mindset.**

Your approach, resilience, and **business strategy** will determine your success more than anything else.

That's why in **Chapter 1**, we're starting with the **most critical factor in self-publishing success:** your **mindset.**

Are you ready to think like a **successful author-preneur?**

Let's begin.

1. Developing the Right Mindset for Publishing Success

Why Mindset Matters in Self-Publishing

You've finally decided to publish your book. You sit down, start writing, and suddenly—doubt creeps in.

"Will anyone read this? Will it sell? What if this whole thing is a waste of time?"

You're not alone. Every writer, at some point, has these thoughts. The difference between those who **push through** and those who **give up** often comes down to **mindset.**

Even with a brilliant idea, a polished manuscript, and a solid marketing plan, the wrong mindset can lead to **self-sabotage.** But here's the good news: you're in control of your outlook. You can **train yourself to think like a successful author**—one who overcomes obstacles, adapts to change, and keeps moving forward.

This chapter will help you develop the right mindset for long-term success. We'll cover:

- Why treating self-publishing as a **business** is essential.
- How to **stay resilient** in the face of setbacks.
- The importance of **consistency and patience** in building your author career.
- Practical ways to **overcome self-doubt and fear of failure.**

By the end, you'll have a solid foundation for success—one that will help you stay committed, confident, and focused on your goals.

"The worst enemy to creativity is self-doubt."

— Sylvia Plath

SHIFTING TO A GROWTH MINDSET

Many new authors assume that success in self-publishing comes down to **natural talent** or **luck**. In reality, it's about growth. The most successful authors are those who **learn, adapt, and improve over time.**

A **growth mindset** means:

- Understanding that **skills can be developed**—writing, marketing, and publishing are all learnable.
- Seeing **challenges as opportunities** rather than roadblocks.
- Recognizing that **failure isn't final**—it's just part of the learning process.

Contrast this with a **fixed mindset**, where people believe that if they're not immediately good at something, they never will be.

That kind of thinking holds authors back from reaching their full potential.

Publishing your first book might not go exactly as planned. Maybe sales are slow, or your marketing efforts don't take off right away. That's okay. Every mistake is an opportunity to learn and improve.

THE ENTREPRENEURIAL APPROACH TO WRITING

Self-publishing isn't just about writing—it's about running a business. If you want to **make money from your books,** you need to think beyond creativity and embrace the **business side of publishing.**

That means:

- **Seeing your book as a product.** It's not just words on a page; it's something people will buy. You need to consider **cover design, formatting, and positioning** in the market.
- **Understanding your audience.** Who are your readers? What are they looking for? Successful authors tailor their work to **serve their audience,** not just themselves.
- **Being strategic.** Success isn't random. It comes from **planning your publishing schedule, marketing efforts, and long-term goals.**
- **Experimenting and adapting.** You might have to test different genres, cover styles, price points, or advertising strategies before finding what works best for you.

Many self-published authors start **with no budget** and learn as they go. Others **invest in tools and services** to speed up the process. Either way, the key is to **treat it like a business, not a hobby.**

Thinking like an entrepreneur allows you to **work smarter**, not harder. It helps you create **sustainable success** instead of relying on short-term luck.

Overcoming Self-Doubt and Fear of Failure

One of the biggest challenges new authors face isn't **learning how to publish**—it's believing in themselves enough to **follow through**.

The fear of failure stops countless writers from ever hitting "publish."

Doubt is normal. But if you let it control you, it will **paralyze** your progress. Here's how to push past it:

- **Start small.** Instead of thinking about the entire publishing process, focus on one step at a time. Write the next chapter. Edit one section. Design your book cover. Small actions build momentum.
- **Accept imperfection.** No book is perfect. Don't let the fear of "not being good enough" keep you from publishing. Many successful authors improve over time —not before they release their first book.
- **Get feedback.** Join writing communities, work with beta readers, or hire an editor. **Honest feedback builds confidence** and improves your work.
- **Celebrate milestones.** Finishing your first draft? That's a win. Publishing your book? Huge achievement. Every step forward matters.

You will make mistakes. Everyone does. The key is to **keep moving forward** anyway.

Mindset Resources for Success

Developing a **strong author mindset** takes time, but these resources can help:

Books

- *The War of Art* – Steven Pressfield (*Overcoming creative resistance and self-doubt*)
- *Atomic Habits* – James Clear (*Developing consistent, productive writing habits*)
- *The $100 Startup* – Chris Guillebeau (*Thinking like an entrepreneur with limited resources*)

Podcasts & YouTube Channels

- *The Self-Publishing School Podcast* – Practical publishing and marketing insights.
- *The Creative Penn Podcast* – Writing, publishing, and business strategies.
- *The Smart Passive Income Podcast* – How to build multiple income streams from your work.

These resources reinforce **the power of persistence, strategy, and mindset**—all crucial for a long-term publishing career.

Summary: Laying the Mental Foundation for Publishing Success

Self-publishing is a journey. It's not about getting lucky or having the perfect book from day one. **It's about learning, adapting, and consistently improving.**

To recap:

- **A growth mindset** helps you view setbacks as learning opportunities.
- **Thinking like an entrepreneur** allows you to make smarter publishing decisions.
- **Overcoming self-doubt** is essential—progress beats perfection.
- **Patience and resilience** will set you apart from authors who give up too soon.

Next Steps

Now that you have the **right mindset** in place, it's time to take the next critical step: choosing **the right topic** for your book.

Many new authors dive into writing without first researching whether their book idea has **market demand**. The result? A great book that no one is searching for. To succeed on KDP, you need to strike a balance between **passion and profitability**—a topic that excites you but also has **an audience ready to buy.**

In Chapter 2, we'll walk through the process of **finding the right topic and conducting market research.** You'll learn:

- How to identify **profitable book niches** that align with your interests.
- What tools and strategies help validate **market demand** before you write.
- How to avoid common mistakes that lead to books that don't sell.

By the end of the next chapter, you'll have **clarity and confidence** in your book topic—setting yourself up for success before you even start writing.

2. Finding the Right Topic & Market Research

Why Choosing the Right Niche Matters

You could write the most insightful, well-crafted book in the world—but if no one is looking for it, it won't sell.

Many new authors make the mistake of choosing a book topic based solely on **personal passion**, without considering whether there's **actual demand.** While passion is important, self-publishing is also a business. If your goal is to earn from your books, you need to align your interests with **what readers are actively searching for.**

This chapter will show you how to:

- **Identify** profitable book niches
- **Use data-driven research** to validate demand
- **Avoid common mistakes** that lead to books that don't sell
- **Analyze competition** to spot opportunities

By the end, you'll have a validated book idea that sets you up for success before you even start writing.

> *"Don't focus on having a great idea; focus on solving a real problem for real people."*

— *Seth Godin*

CASE STUDY: NICHE MARKET SUCCESS

Sarah Lee wanted to write a self-help book but knew the competition was fierce. Instead of writing a generic motivation book, she researched underserved niches and found that 'Overcoming Social Anxiety at Work' had high demand but low competition. By optimizing her title and keywords, her book ranked on the first page of Amazon search results and consistently sold over 300 copies per month.

Key Takeaways:

- Micro-niching increases discoverability.
- Market research prevents wasted effort on overly competitive categories.

The key is to **find a niche that balances passion and profitability**:

- A topic that is **too broad** means overwhelming competition.
- A topic that is **too narrow** means limited demand.
- The **sweet spot** is a niche where **readers are actively looking for books**, but competition isn't impossible to break into.

In this chapter, you'll learn:

- How to identify **profitable book niches**
- Tools and strategies to **validate demand** before writing
- How to **analyze competition** and spot opportunities

By the end, you'll have a **data-backed book idea** that has a real shot at success.

TRADITIONAL VS. SELF-PUBLISHING: HOW MARKET RESEARCH DIFFERS

Before diving into research, let's compare how **traditional publishing** and **self-publishing** approach market validation.

Traditional Publishing Process

1. Write a book proposal (or complete manuscript).
2. Query literary agents and wait for responses.
3. If accepted, undergo months (or years) of editing and production.
4. The publisher handles distribution, but the author has little control.
5. Royalties are **low (typically 10-15%)**, and authors often receive advances instead.

Pros: Publishers handle marketing and sales.

Cons: High barriers to entry, slow process, and loss of creative control.

Self-Publishing on KDP

1. **Validate demand before writing** to ensure people want your book.

2. Write and edit at your own pace.
3. Format and publish directly to Amazon **without needing approval.**
4. Set your own pricing and keep **up to 70% royalties.**
5. Market and promote your book using Amazon's platform and external strategies.

Pros: Full control, **higher earnings**, and faster publishing.

Cons: You're responsible for **marketing and audience building.**

With **self-publishing, market research is essential** because you **don't have a publisher handling sales. Your success depends on making smart decisions upfront.**

How to Identify a Profitable Niche

A **niche** is simply a **focused topic.** The more specific you get, the better your chances of success.

Broad vs. Micro-Niche Examples

- **Broad Niche:** Personal Finance
- **Niche:** Budgeting for Beginners
- **Micro-Niche:** Budgeting for Single Moms on a Low Income

The issue with broad niches is **competition.** If you publish a generic book on "fitness," you're competing with thousands of established books. But if you niche down to "bodyweight workouts for busy professionals," you reduce competition while **still reaching a strong audience.**

A strong niche should:

- Have **proven demand** – People are searching for books on this topic.
- Be **low or medium competition** – You don't want to compete with thousands of bestsellers.
- Be **evergreen or have lasting appeal** – A book that remains relevant over time is more valuable.
- Align with your **interest or ability** – Even if hiring a writer, you need to ensure quality.

If a niche meets these criteria, it's **worth pursuing**.

WHICH NICHES ARE PROFITABLE?

While trends shift, the following categories consistently perform well:

Non-Fiction:

- Productivity & Time Management
- Personal Finance & Investing
- Self-Help & Mindset
- Online Business & Side Hustles
- Health & Dieting
- Language Learning
- DIY & Home Improvement

Fiction (Profitable Subgenres):

- Cozy Mysteries
- Romance (Billionaire, Sports, Paranormal, etc.)
- Sci-Fi & Fantasy
- Thriller & Suspense
- Short Story Anthologies

Low-Content Books:

- Planners & Workbooks
- Journals & Logbooks
- Coloring Books (Adults & Kids)
- Activity Books & Puzzle Books

But how do you **know** if a niche is worth pursuing? **That's where research comes in.**

RESEARCHING MARKET DEMAND

Market demand determines whether your book will sell. Instead of guessing, use **data-driven research** to validate a topic before investing time or money into writing.

How to Use the Amazon Best Sellers List

Amazon's Best Sellers Rank (BSR) is a key indicator of how well a book is selling. Every book listed on Amazon has a **BSR number**, which tells you its sales performance relative to other books in its category.

Why is BSR Important?

- It **reveals market demand**—a lower BSR means a book is selling well.
- It helps you **estimate potential earnings** for books in your niche.
- It **shows competition levels**, helping you decide if a niche is worth entering.

How to Use BSR in Market Research

1. **Find Books in Your Niche**
   - Search for a topic on **Amazon Kindle Store** (e.g., "Productivity," "Budgeting," or "Journaling").
   - Look at the **top-ranking books** in that niche.

2. **Check Their BSR Numbers**
   - Scroll down to the **"Product Details"** section of a book's listing.
   - The BSR is listed under **"Amazon Best Sellers Rank."**
3. **Estimate Sales Using BSR**
   - A book ranked **#1 - 10,000** in the Kindle Store is selling **very well** (potentially hundreds of copies daily).
   - A book ranked **10,000 - 50,000** is selling consistently (likely 1-10 copies per day).
   - A book ranked **100,000+** is selling occasionally, but might not be profitable.
4. **Compare BSR Across Multiple Books**
   - If **multiple books in your niche have a BSR under 50,000**, it means there's strong demand.
   - If most books are **ranked 300,000+**, it may indicate weak demand.
5. **Look for Gaps in the Market**
   - If you find books with **high BSR (good sales) but poor covers or bad reviews**, it's an opportunity to create something better.
   - If a niche has **only a few successful books**, you might have an easier time ranking.

Example of Using BSR for Research

Suppose you're considering writing a book on **"Decluttering for Beginners."**

- You check Amazon and find several books ranked **10,000 - 30,000 BSR**—a great sign of demand.
- The books with high rankings have **good covers and reviews**, meaning competition is strong.

- You also find books ranked around **250,000 BSR**—these may be struggling due to poor quality or weak marketing.

This data helps you decide whether **"Decluttering for Beginners" is a viable niche** or if you should refine your topic to something more specific (e.g., "Decluttering for Busy Parents").

BSR is **always changing**, so check rankings over a few days to get a more accurate picture of a niche's potential. Combining **BSR analysis with KD Pilot and Publisher Rocket** gives you the best insights into market demand.

Google Trends

- Go to <u>Google Trends</u> and enter your topic.
- Look for **steady or rising search interest**—if it's declining, it may not be worth pursuing.
- Compare different keywords to see which version of a topic is more popular.

Reddit & Quora

- Search for your topic on forums like Reddit and Quora.
- Are people **asking questions** about it? Active discussion = real-world demand.
- Look for **gaps**—if many people are asking, but few books exist, it's a golden opportunity.

Advanced Research: Market Demand & Competitive Analysis

If you're serious about treating self-publishing as a **business,** invest in **market research tools** that give deeper insights into profitability.

Publisher Rocket – Best for Keyword & Category Research

- Shows **search volume** for book topics.
- Reveals **estimated monthly sales** of top books in your niche.
- Helps pick **keywords** that increase discoverability.
- Finds **low-competition categories** where you can rank as a bestseller.

How to Use Publisher Rocket:

- Type a keyword into the **Keyword Search** tool.
- Look at the **monthly searches** and **competition score**.
- Find categories where books **rank but don't have too many competitors**.

Pro Tip: Pick a niche where books are selling **500+ copies per month** but **don't have thousands of competing titles.**

KDSpy – Best for Sales & Revenue Analysis

- Shows the **BSR** of books in any niche.
- Estimates **monthly earnings** of top books.
- Helps spot **niches with steady sales over time.**

How to Use KDSpy:

- Open Amazon and go to a book category.
- Click the KDSpy extension.
- Look at the **sales data** to see if books are consistently selling.

Pro Tip: If books in a niche make **$1,000+ per month** consistently, it's **worth exploring.**

Other Competitor Tools to Consider:

- **Helium 10** – Advanced keyword tracking for Amazon.
- **KDP Champ** – Detailed book performance tracking.
- **BookBeam** – Helps find profitable book niches.

Each tool has different strengths, but all help **reduce guesswork** in choosing a **profitable niche**.

FINAL VALIDATION CHECKLIST: DOES YOUR IDEA HOLD UP?

Before committing to your book topic, ask yourself:

- **Is there a clear audience for this book?**
- **Are multiple books in this niche making steady sales?**
- **Is there a gap you can fill—either in content, presentation, or depth?**
- **Are people actively searching for this topic?** (Use Google Trends, Amazon, and keyword tools.)
- **Does this topic excite you enough to stay committed?**

If your book idea **meets these criteria**, you're **ready to move forward** with outlining and writing.

NEXT STEPS: CREATING A WINNING OUTLINE

Now that you've validated your book idea, it's time to **structure your content for success**. A well-organized outline makes the **writing process easier**, improves readability, and ensures your book **delivers real value**.

In **Chapter 3**, we'll cover:

- How to **structure your book logically**

- Different **outlining techniques** for fiction and non-fiction
- The benefits of **AI-assisted outlining vs. manual**

By the end of the next chapter, you'll have a **clear roadmap** for your book—setting you up for a **smooth writing process**.

3. Outlining Your Book

Why Outlining Matters

Once you've identified a profitable niche, the next step is to create a detailed outline for your book. A strong outline not only streamlines the writing process but also improves the **marketability** of your book. A well-structured book enhances **reader retention**, encourages **positive reviews,** and ultimately **boosts sales rankings** on platforms like Amazon.

Outlining your book before writing has several benefits:

- **Saves time** – A clear structure makes the writing process faster and more efficient.
- **Improves clarity** – Ensures your ideas are presented in a logical and coherent way.
- **Prevents writer's block** – Gives you a clear direction, reducing uncertainty during writing.
- **Helps with editing** – A well-structured book is easier to revise and refine.
- **Enhances marketing & positioning** – Helps identify key themes for your book's description and keywords.

This chapter explores two approaches to outlining: **manual outlining and AI-assisted outlining.** Both methods have their advantages, and combining them can be the most effective strategy.

> *"I always have a basic plot outline, but I like to leave some things to be decided while I write. It's more fun that way. However, I couldn't function without an outline."*
>
> *– J.K. Rowling*

OUTLINING YOUR BOOK

Creating an outline manually allows for **deeper thought and originality.** Here's a simple method to structure your book from scratch:

1. Start with a Working Title

Your title should be clear, specific, and **keyword-friendly.** It doesn't have to be final but should reflect the book's main topic and attract potential readers.

2. Break the Topic into Major Sections (Chapters)

- Identify the **main themes or sections** that need to be covered.
- Consider what the reader **expects to learn** and in what order.

3. List Subtopics Under Each Chapter

- Within each chapter, break things down into **smaller sections or key points.**

- Ask yourself: **What must be included for this chapter to be complete?**

4. Use Visual Tools for Organization

- **Mind Maps** – Great for brainstorming and visually connecting ideas.
- **Index Cards** – Useful for rearranging topics and structuring flow.

5. Review & Organize the Structure

- Does the order make sense?
- Are there any **gaps in the information**?
- Will the reader **progress smoothly** from one chapter to the next?

6. Refine & Expand the Outline

- Add bullet points or **brief descriptions** to each section.
- If needed, research other books or articles to **ensure completeness.**

Taking the time to manually outline your book will make the writing process **faster and more efficient** later on.

OUTLINING YOUR BOOK WITH AI

AI tools can **speed up** the outlining process, but they should be used strategically—not as a replacement for **thoughtful planning.** Here's how to use AI effectively:

1. Generate an Initial Outline

Use a tool like **ChatGPT, Claude AI, or Notion AI** to suggest a book outline. Provide specific input such as:

- *"Create an outline for a non-fiction book on [your topic]."*
- *"Generate 10 chapter ideas for a book about [niche]."*

2. Refine & Customize the Outline

- AI-generated outlines **often need adjustments** to fit your vision.
- Rearrange sections, remove irrelevant points, and **add missing elements.**

3. Use AI for Expanding on Sections

If a chapter feels thin, ask AI to **suggest subtopics or key details.**

- Example: *"What are common beginner mistakes in [topic]?"*

4. Be Aware of AI Limitations

- AI-generated outlines can be **generic or repetitive.**
- AI may reflect **biases based on available data,** so fact-check recommendations.
- **Critical thinking is essential**—use AI as a **brainstorming tool, not a final decision-maker.**

WHICH APPROACH IS BEST?

- If you have **strong knowledge of your topic,** creating your own outline ensures **originality and depth.**
- If you struggle with **structuring ideas,** AI can provide a **starting point to refine.**

- **The ideal method combines both:** AI for brainstorming, then **manual adjustments** for clarity and purpose.

ADDITIONAL READING & RESEARCH

For those looking to improve their outlining skills, consider the following resources:

Books

- *Save the Cat! Writes a Novel* – Jessica Brody (*for structuring stories*)
- *Outlining Your Novel* – K.M. Weiland (*deep dive into manual outlining*)
- *The Snowflake Method* – Randy Ingermanson (*for methodical planning*)

Online Resources

- The Kindlepreneur Blog (*excellent for market-driven outlining*)
- The Self-Publishing School Website (*step-by-step guides on book planning*)
- YouTube Channels – *Chris Fox Writes, Reedsy* (*for in-depth tutorials*)

NEXT STEPS

By now, you should have a **solid, well-structured outline**, ready to move into the **writing phase**—whether you're doing it yourself, using AI assistance, or outsourcing to a **ghostwriter**.

A **strong outline** serves as the foundation for a book that is **clear, engaging, and marketable**.

In **Chapter 4**, we'll explore the **writing process itself**, including:

- How to **write efficiently** and maintain productivity.
- Choosing between **writing yourself, using AI, or hiring a ghostwriter.**
- Overcoming **writer's block** and staying consistent.
- Editing strategies to **refine your first draft.**

By the end of the next chapter, you'll know **exactly how to turn your outline into a full manuscript** without getting stuck.

4. Writing Your First Kindle Book

Choosing Your Path

Every successful book starts with a single sentence. But how do you turn that sentence into a **well-structured, compelling book?** That's what this chapter will help you achieve.

Writing your first book can feel **overwhelming**, but it's also one of the most **exciting** parts of self-publishing. Whether you are:

- Developing your own ideas,
- Leveraging AI tools to assist, or
- Outsourcing to a ghostwriter,

There are multiple ways to **complete your manuscript.** The key is to **stay focused, maintain a clear vision, and understand the process** so that you can move from concept to finished book without getting stuck.

This chapter explores **various writing approaches,** including how to:

- Write efficiently and **maintain quality.**
- **Overcome writer's block** and **stay productive.**
- **Decide whether to write, use AI tools, or hire a ghostwriter.**

Whether you have the time to write your book yourself or need **assistance**, this chapter will help you **navigate the journey.**

"Almost all good writing begins with terrible first efforts. You need to start somewhere."

— Anne Lamott

COMPARISON: FAST VS. SLOW PUBLISHING SUCCESS

- **Alex** writes using dictation software, publishing a 40,000-word book every two months. By releasing multiple books quickly, he maximized earnings through Amazon's algorithm, generating $5,000/month.
- **Emma**, a literary fiction author, spent two years crafting her book but leveraged preorders and marketing to launch successfully, leading to long-term consistent sales.

Key Takeaways:

- Rapid publishing benefits short-term gains.
- Slow, high-quality publishing builds longevity and brand reputation.

If you've always wanted to be a **published author**, writing your own book can be a fulfilling experience. The key to success is **establishing a writing habit and maintaining momentum**.

Finding Your Writing Flow

- **Set realistic goals** – Avoid feeling overwhelmed by thinking you need to write the entire book in one sitting. Break it down into manageable chunks, such as writing for **30 minutes a day** or completing a chapter per week.
- **Minimize distractions** – Turn off notifications, set your phone aside, and create a **dedicated writing space** to maintain focus.
- **Write first, edit later** – Many new authors slow their progress by editing as they go. Instead, focus on **getting your ideas down first**, then revise later.

Overcoming Writer's Block

Writer's block is something even seasoned authors face. Later in this book, we'll explore it in more detail, but here are a few **quick strategies** to push through:

- **Freewriting** – Set a timer for 10 minutes and write without stopping or worrying about quality. This helps clear mental fog.
- **Change your environment** – Sometimes, a **fresh setting** can spark creativity.
- **Take breaks** – Stepping away from your manuscript for a **short walk or a day off** can help you return with fresh ideas.

Efficient Writing and Maintaining Momentum

- **Break the task into smaller goals** – Whether writing alone or collaborating, focus on completing **one section at a time.**
- **Set deadlines and stick to them** – Use a **planner** to schedule deadlines for writing, editing, and final revisions.
- **Maintain balance** – Avoid burnout by taking **scheduled breaks** and not obsessing over perfection.

Editing and Revisions

Once you have a **first draft**, it's time to **refine your work.** The **editing phase** is where your book **evolves** into something polished and professional.

Focus Areas in Editing:

- **Structure and organization** – Does the content **flow logically?**
- **Grammar and spelling** – Use tools like **Grammarly** or **ProWritingAid** to catch errors, but always review your manuscript manually.
- **Clarity and style** – Are there areas where your writing can be **more concise or engaging?**

Good editing takes multiple rounds, so don't rush the process.

Leveraging AI to Speed Up the Writing Process

If you're **short on time,** AI can be an **excellent assistant.** However, **AI should enhance your writing, not replace it.**

Using AI for Idea Generation and Outlining

AI tools like **ChatGPT, Claude, or Jasper** can help:

- **Generate chapter outlines** based on your topic.
- **Expand on specific sections** of your book.
- **Provide writing prompts** to keep your content flowing.

This is particularly useful for **overcoming writer's block** or **structuring your ideas.**

AI-Assisted Writing Tools

There are several AI-powered writing assistants that can **streamline your workflow:**

- **Sudowrite** – Best for fiction, generating dialogue, scenes, and character development.
- **Jasper** – Great for non-fiction, turning outlines into **well-structured chapters.**
- **Frase** – Helps with **research and creating SEO-friendly** non-fiction content.

Pros and Cons of AI-Assisted Writing

Pros:

- Saves time by quickly **generating text and ideas.**
- Helps **structure your book efficiently.**
- Useful for **overcoming writer's block.**

Cons:

- AI-generated content can feel **generic** and lack **personality.**
- Requires **human revision** to maintain authenticity and clarity.
- Can introduce **factual inaccuracies** if not properly reviewed.

AI is a powerful tool, but it works best when combined with **your own expertise and personal touch.**

Hiring a Ghostwriter: When to Consider It

For some, the writing process is **too time-consuming or challenging.** Hiring a **ghostwriter** can be a **great solution,** but it's important to ensure you're **choosing the right one.**

When to Hire a Ghostwriter

- **You're short on time** – If you want to **publish quickly** but can't commit to writing, a ghostwriter can help.
- **You lack writing experience** – If structuring a book feels **overwhelming,** a professional can bring your ideas to life.
- **You want a high-quality product** – A skilled ghostwriter ensures your content is **polished and engaging.**

Where to Find a Good Ghostwriter

- **Upwork** – A marketplace for freelancers with experience in various niches.
- **Reedsy** – Connects authors with vetted ghostwriters.
- **Scripted & WriterAccess** – Platforms that offer access to **professional writers** for book projects.

What to Expect from a Ghostwriter

- **Pricing** – Expect to pay **$800-$1,500 for a non-fiction book,** with fiction often costing more.
- **Communication** – Provide a **clear outline** and maintain regular check-ins to ensure the final product meets your expectations.

The Hybrid Approach: Combining AI and Ghostwriting

Some authors find a **hybrid approach** most effective. This can include:

- **Using AI to generate an outline.**
- **Hiring a ghostwriter to draft the book.**
- **Refining and editing with AI tools.**

Example of a Hybrid Workflow:

1. **Use ChatGPT** to generate a detailed **chapter outline.**
2. **Hire a ghostwriter** to write the book based on the AI-generated structure.
3. **Utilize AI tools** like Grammarly or Sudowrite for **post-draft editing and refinement.**

This approach allows for **efficiency without compromising quality.**

Next Steps

Writing a book is a journey, and the path you take will depend on your **goals, time, and resources.** Whether you choose to:

- Write the book yourself,
- Leverage AI tools,
- Hire a ghostwriter, or
- Use a hybrid approach,

The **most important factors** are **consistency, quality, and strategic execution.**

Beyond writing your own books, **offering a guided writing service** can open up new opportunities, allowing you to **help others while building a sustainable business** in the self-publishing industry.

In **Chapter 5,** we'll take this concept further—**exploring how to turn your guided writing service into a profitable business model.** You'll learn how to:

- **Package your expertise.**
- **Attract clients.**
- **Create scalable income streams** that go beyond just publishing your own books.

5. Helping Others Publish – Turning Book Creation Into a Business

Why Some People Need Your Help to Publish

Every expert has valuable knowledge, but not everyone knows how to turn that knowledge into a book. **That's where you step in.**

Many professionals—**business owners, consultants, speakers, and coaches**—have valuable insights to share but lack the **time, writing skills, or knowledge of the publishing process.** Some have been told by clients, *"You should write a book!"* but don't know where to start.

By offering a **guided writing and publishing service,** you can help these individuals **transform their expertise into a published book,** all while **building your own business** in the process. Thanks to **AI tools and self-publishing platforms,** it's easier than ever to **assist others in writing and publishing** without needing a **full team of editors and ghostwriters.**

"The role of a writer is not to say what we all can say, but what we are unable to say."

— Anaïs Nin

CASE STUDY: LISA, THE LEADERSHIP COACH

Lisa, a corporate leadership coach, had been running workshops for years, helping mid-level managers improve their leadership skills. **Her clients frequently asked if she had a book** they could reference after the sessions. However, she was too busy running her business to write one.

When she finally published, the book did more than generate royalties—it led to:

- **Higher-priced consulting gigs**
- **Keynote speaking invitations**
- **An online course that expanded her business beyond one-on-one coaching**

This is why books matter and why professionals will **pay for help** in creating them.

THE BIGGER PICTURE: BOOKS AS BUSINESS ASSETS

For many professionals, a book isn't just about selling copies—it's **a marketing tool, a lead magnet, and a stepping stone** to bigger opportunities.

Key Benefits for Professionals

- **Credibility Boost** – A book solidifies authority in a given field.

- **Marketing Leverage** – Books generate **leads and attract clients.**
- **Passive Income Stream** – Selling books can add an additional **revenue stream.**
- **Business Growth** – Books help professionals scale their influence through **speaking gigs, partnerships, and online courses.**

By helping professionals publish, you're **not just creating books —you're helping them build their brand, business, and income.**

Who Can Benefit from a Guided Book Writing Service?

Not everyone needs to write a book, but for **the right people**, it can be a **game-changer.**

Coaches, Trainers, and Consultants

A book helps them **establish credibility, differentiate themselves from competitors, and attract more clients.**

Example: Mark, a fitness coach specializing in training older adults, turned his methodology into a book on **fitness for people over 50.** The book not only sold well but also **drove traffic to his online coaching program,** increasing his high-paying clients.

Public Speakers & Industry Experts

For those already **speaking publicly,** a book extends their reach, allowing them to **connect with a broader audience beyond event attendees.**

Entrepreneurs & Business Owners

A book can act as a **powerful business card,** helping them secure **clients, investors, or partnerships.**

Example: Daniel, a small business owner, wrote a book about **affordable digital marketing strategies**. Instead of focusing on book sales, he used the book to **attract ideal clients**, positioning himself as an **expert in his industry**.

If someone has **valuable knowledge** but doesn't have time to **write and publish**, they **need** your services.

How the Process Works: Helping Someone Publish Their Book

Step 1: The Consultation – Identifying the Book's Purpose

Before diving in, it's crucial to define:

- **The author's goal** – Is the book meant to **generate income, attract clients, or establish authority?**
- **The target audience** – A **leadership book for executives** differs from one for **first-time managers.**
- **Existing content** – Does the author have **drafts, notes, or just an idea?**

Example: A real estate investor had **over 100 pages of notes, voice recordings, and blog posts** but no structure. He needed help **organizing his ideas into a logical, reader-friendly flow.**

Step 2: Creating a Strong Outline

Many professionals struggle to write because **they don't know where to start.** AI tools like **ChatGPT** can help generate an outline (**see Chapter 3**), but refining it based on the author's **expertise** is essential.

Example: A life coach wanted to write about **self-discipline.** Instead of listing generic tips, the outline was structured around:

- **Case studies**

- Step-by-step exercises
- A 90-day action plan

A well-structured book makes **writing (or dictation) much easier and faster.**

Step 3: Writing – AI-Assisted, Ghostwriting, or Coaching?

Depending on their **preference and budget**, clients can choose:

- **AI-Assisted Writing** – Using tools like **ChatGPT** to create drafts, later refined for clarity and voice.
- **Ghostwriting** – You (or a hired writer) craft the book based on **interviews and notes.**
- **Writing Coaching** – The client writes while you provide **structure, feedback, and revisions.**

The **right approach** depends on how involved the client wants to be in the process.

Step 4: Editing, Formatting & Cover Design

Once the book is written, it needs **polishing**. Clients may require guidance on:

- **Editing tools** like Grammarly or ProWritingAid.
- **Formatting for Kindle & print** using Reedsy, Vellum, or Word.
- **Cover design** through Fiverr, BookBrush, or Canva.

Even if the content is **solid**, a **poorly formatted book with an amateur cover** will not sell well.

Step 5: Publishing & Marketing Strategy

Uploading the book to **KDP** is straightforward, but **marketing is where clients often need the most help.** You can guide them on:

- Amazon categories & keywords – Ensuring they **reach the right audience.**
- **Building an email list or social media audience before launch.**
- **Using their book to drive traffic to their business or service.**

Example: A career coach used his book to **launch a paid membership site** for job seekers, leveraging the book as a **gateway to his premium services.**

A book is **only as successful as its marketing strategy.**

How to Find Clients for This Service

Network in Business Circles

LinkedIn, Facebook groups, and industry events are filled with **professionals who want to publish but don't know where to start. Position yourself as the go-to expert.**

Offer a Free Consultation or Webinar

- Host a **"How to Publish Your First Book"** webinar.
- Provide a **free consultation** to assess potential clients' needs.

Partner with Business Coaches & Consultants

Many business coaches want books but **lack time to write.** Offer to **co-create books** with them as part of their programs.

Business Model & Pricing Considerations

If you're serious about turning this into a **profitable business,** you need a **structured pricing model.**

- **Flat Fee Per Project** – Charge **$2,000–$10,000** depending on complexity.
- **Hourly Consulting Fees** – Offer coaching at **$100–$300 per hour.**
- **Revenue Share** – Take a percentage of **book sales.**

Scaling your business can involve:

- Hiring **additional ghostwriters.**
- Offering **DIY book creation courses.**
- Providing **done-for-you publishing packages.**

NEXT STEPS: CREATING A SUSTAINABLE PUBLISHING BUSINESS

Helping others publish books isn't just about **writing**—it's about offering a **service-based business around publishing expertise.**

By mastering the **art of guided book creation**, you're not just helping others—you're **building a sustainable, high-value business** in the publishing industry.

In **Chapter 6**, we'll cover **formatting and preparing your book** for Kindle publishing, ensuring **it meets professional standards** before going live.

6. Formatting and Preparing Your Book for Kindle Publishing

Understanding the Basics of Book Formatting

When publishing a book on Amazon Kindle, ensuring your manuscript is properly formatted is one of the most crucial steps. Whether you're releasing an eBook, paperback, or hardcover, proper formatting guarantees your book will be **readable, professional, and visually appealing** across various devices and in print. A well-formatted book not only enhances the reader experience but also contributes to **positive reviews, increased credibility, and greater sales.**

Improper formatting can lead to **text running off the page, inconsistent fonts, or awkward page breaks**—issues that can frustrate readers and result in negative reviews. By following proper formatting techniques, you can avoid these pitfalls and ensure a polished, professional presentation.

In this chapter, we'll guide you through the formatting process, starting with **eBooks**, then moving on to **paperback and hardcover formats**. While each format has unique requirements, the principles of good formatting remain consistent, making the process easier. We'll also introduce **both free and premium tools** that can streamline formatting.

Be sure to refer to the **detailed resources provided by KDP (Kindle Direct Publishing)** for specific formatting guidelines, available in their Help Center.

"A poorly formatted book is like a beautiful song played out of tune—it distracts from the message and diminishes the experience."

— Joel Friedlander

FORMATTING YOUR EBOOK FOR KINDLE

Why Proper Formatting Matters

Proper eBook formatting ensures your book looks professional on **all Kindle devices**—including Kindle Paperwhite, Fire tablets, and the Kindle app on smartphones and tablets. If your manuscript isn't formatted correctly, it can lead to **poor layout, broken chapter flows, or unreadable text**—all of which can hurt your book's reputation and sales potential.

STEP-BY-STEP EBOOK FORMATTING

Accepted File Formats by KDP

KDP accepts three primary file types for eBook publishing:

- **DOCX:** The standard Word document, widely compatible and easy to work with.
- **EPUB:** The preferred format for reflowable text, ensuring the best compatibility across all Kindle devices.

- **KPF (Kindle Create File):** Optimized for Kindle devices when using Kindle Create for formatting.

While KDP allows multiple file formats, **EPUB is the industry standard** for reflowable text and offers the best flexibility for formatting across different Kindle devices.

You can format your book using programs like **Word, Google Docs, or Pages**, but for a more polished look, specialized tools are recommended:

- **Scrivener:** A powerful tool for organizing and drafting your manuscript, with export options for Kindle-ready formats.
- **Reedsy Book Editor:** A free, web-based tool that automatically formats manuscripts into professional eBook files.
- **Vellum:** A premium formatting tool that offers high-quality templates for both eBooks and print books.

Preparing Your Manuscript for Kindle

Follow these simple formatting guidelines to ensure your eBook meets KDP's standards:

- **Font & Size:** Use readable fonts like **Arial or Georgia** at **12 pt.**
- **Line Spacing:** Use **1.5 or double-spacing** for readability.
- **Margins:** Set **1-inch margins** to prevent text from appearing too close to the edges.
- **Headings:** Apply **Heading 1 for chapter titles** for automatic table of contents generation.
- **Page Breaks:** Insert **page breaks** after each chapter for smooth transitions.

- **Save Format:** Before uploading, save your manuscript as **DOCX, RTF, or EPUB.**

FORMATTING YOUR PAPERBACK AND HARDCOVER BOOKS

Key Differences Between eBook and Print Formatting

Unlike eBooks, **paperbacks and hardcovers require a fixed layout,** meaning you must precisely format **page size, margins, and spacing.** The layout you create will be exactly how it appears in print.

Choosing the Right Trim Size & Layout for Print

Your book's **trim size** determines its final dimensions after printing. KDP offers several options, with the most popular being:

- **5" x 8"** – Ideal for fiction and smaller non-fiction books.
- **6" x 9"** – The standard size for trade paperbacks and most non-fiction books.
- **8.5" x 11"** – Best for workbooks, planners, or textbooks.

Selecting the right size depends on **your genre, audience, and market expectations.**

Print Formatting Guidelines

To create a professional paperback or hardcover, follow these guidelines:

Margins & Bleed:

- Standard margins should be **at least 0.5"** on all sides.
- For books over **300 pages**, increase the **inner margin (gutter)** for better readability.

- If your book includes **full-page images or colored elements**, enable **bleed settings**; otherwise, select "No Bleed" in KDP's print settings.

Font & Line Spacing for Print:

- Use **serif fonts** (e.g., **Garamond, Minion Pro, Georgia, Times New Roman**) for better readability in print.
- Font size should be **11pt to 12pt** for body text and **14pt to 16pt** for chapter titles.
- Line spacing should be **1.2 to 1.5** for optimal readability.

Print File Submission:

- Unlike eBooks, print books require a **PDF file** to ensure text and design elements remain consistent.
- Ensure your manuscript is formatted for **the correct trim size** before converting it to PDF.

Cover Design Considerations

For **paperback and hardcover books**, you need a **full-cover design**, including **the front cover, spine, and back cover.**

KDP's **Cover Calculator tool** helps you generate the exact dimensions based on **trim size and page count.** You can also use design tools like **Canva or BookBrush,** or hire a professional cover designer.

Tools for Formatting Print Books

Several tools make print formatting easier:

- **Scrivener:** Exports PDFs with customizable page sizes.

- **Reedsy Book Editor:** Generates print-ready PDFs that meet KDP's specifications.
- **Vellum:** A premium tool that simplifies both eBook and print formatting.

FRONT AND BACK MATTER

Regardless of format, well-structured **front and back matter** enhance the professionalism of your book.

Front Matter (Before the Main Text)

- **Title Page** – Includes the book title, author name, and subtitle (if applicable).
- **Copyright Page** – Contains copyright details, edition information, and ISBN (if applicable).
- **Table of Contents (TOC)** – Useful for eBooks but optional for print books.

Back Matter (After the Main Content)

- **About the Author** – A short bio with links to your website or other books.
- **Call to Action (CTA)** – Encourage readers to **leave a review, join your email list, or explore your other books.**

For eBooks, ensure **hyperlinks are functional** for easy navigation. For print books, follow KDP's spacing and layout guidelines.

CONVERTING YOUR MANUSCRIPT FOR KDP

Once your manuscript is formatted, convert it for **submission to KDP:**

- **For eBooks** – Save as **DOCX, EPUB, or KPF.**
- **For Print Books** – Upload as a **PDF** with embedded fonts.

Exporting a Print-Ready PDF

- **Microsoft Word:** *Save As* → *PDF* → *Select "Best for Printing."*
- **Google Docs:** *Download As* → *PDF Document.*
- **Scrivener or Vellum:** *Export using KDP's recommended PDF settings.*

Before finalizing, use **KDP Print Previewer** to check your book's layout and correct any formatting errors.

NEXT STEPS

Formatting is a crucial step in the publishing process, but **it doesn't have to be overwhelming.** Whether you're preparing for eBook or print, tools like **Scrivener, Reedsy, and Vellum** will help ensure your book looks professional.

While proper formatting ensures a smooth reading experience, **your book's cover is what catches a reader's eye first.** In the next chapter, we'll explore how to **design a compelling book cover** that stands out in the crowded Kindle marketplace—whether you create it yourself or work with a professional designer.

7. Designing a Professional Book Cover

The Importance of a Great Book Cover

In a marketplace filled with thousands of books, your cover is the **first—and sometimes only—chance** to grab a reader's attention. A poorly designed cover can make even the best-written book go unnoticed, while a professional, genre-appropriate design can boost **visibility and sales.**

Your book cover is often the **first impression** a potential reader has of your book. It's what will either **catch their eye** or cause them to scroll past. Whether you're publishing an **eBook** or a **print edition**, a professional cover is essential for standing out in a crowded marketplace.

A well-designed cover does more than look good—it **conveys the essence of your book and its genre.** In this chapter, we'll explore the key elements of an attractive book cover and give you practical advice on designing one, whether you're doing it yourself or hiring a professional designer.

"A great book cover doesn't just sell the story; it sets the tone for the reader's entire experience."

— Joanna Penn

KEY ELEMENTS OF AN EFFECTIVE BOOK COVER

A great book cover isn't just about being visually appealing; it must **communicate the book's message and attract the right audience.** Here are the main components to consider:

- **Title and Author Name:** These should be **prominent and legible at any size**, especially as thumbnails in online marketplaces.
- **Typography:** Choose fonts that match your genre. For example, **serif fonts** for a more serious tone, or **playful, handwritten fonts** for a lighthearted or fantasy novel.
- **Color Scheme:** Colors evoke emotions. Ensure your **color palette aligns with the mood and genre** of your book.
- **Imagery:** Whether it's a **photo, an abstract design, or an illustration**, it should be high quality and relevant to your book's themes or tone.
- **Branding:** Consider how your cover ties into your **author brand.** If you're writing a **series**, maintaining consistency across covers helps readers instantly recognize your books.

TOOLS FOR DESIGNING YOUR BOOK COVER

You have several options when it comes to creating your book cover—whether you're doing it yourself or outsourcing. Here are some of the most popular tools and services available:

- **KDP Cover Creator:** A free tool from KDP that offers **templates for eBook and print covers.** Great for beginners looking for a simple, professional solution.
- **Canva:** A user-friendly design tool with **pre-made templates, fonts, images, and customization options.** Available in **free and paid versions.**
- **BookBrush:** A platform **specifically designed for authors,** offering easy-to-use templates for **both eBook and print covers.**
- **Vellum:** Primarily a formatting tool, but also includes **basic cover design features** for a polished look.
- **Professional Designers:** If you want a truly custom cover, hiring a designer might be the best option. Platforms like **99designs, Fiverr, and Reedsy** connect you with experienced designers.

EBOOK VS. PRINT BOOK COVERS: KEY DIFFERENCES

While the principles of good cover design apply to both **eBooks and print books,** there are some key differences to keep in mind:

eBook Covers

- **Smaller Size Matters:** eBook covers appear as **thumbnails** in online stores, so they must be **legible and eye-catching at a small size.**
- **KDP Recommended Dimensions:** 2,560 x 1,600 pixels (1.6:1 aspect ratio).
- **File Format:** JPEG or TIFF.
- **Reader Expectations:** Online shoppers often make **snap judgments** based on the cover alone, so clarity and boldness are key.

Print Book Covers

- **Full Wrap Design:** Unlike eBooks, print books require a front cover, spine, and back cover.
- **Trim Size Considerations:** The cover size depends on the **trim size** (e.g., 6" x 9" for trade paperbacks), plus the **spine width** (which varies based on page count).
- **File Format:** Submitted as a **PDF**, at **300 DPI resolution** for high-quality printing.
- **Bleed Requirement:** If the cover extends to the edges of the page, include a **0.125-inch bleed** on all sides.
- **Reader Expectations:** Print buyers evaluate **spine design, back cover content, and overall print quality** more closely.

For precise measurements, use **KDP's Cover Template Generator** to get exact dimensions based on your book's page count and trim size.

DIY vs. Hiring a Professional Cover Designer

The choice between **designing your cover yourself or hiring a professional** depends on **your budget, skills, and time.**

DIY Cover Design

Best for authors who have **design experience or a clear vision** for their book.

- More **affordable** than hiring a designer.
- Full **creative control** over the process.
- Risk of looking **amateurish** if not done well.
- Requires **learning design tools** like Canva or Photoshop.
- A common mistake among DIY designers is **using too many fonts,** which can make the cover look cluttered and unprofessional. Stick to **one or two complementary fonts** for consistency and readability.

Hiring a Professional Designer

Ensures a **polished, high-quality** cover.

- Designers **understand market trends** and genre expectations.
- Saves **time and effort** so you can focus on writing.
- More **expensive** (anywhere from $50 to $500+).
- Less **control** over revisions unless clearly communicated.

For **budget-friendly professional covers,** look at **Fiverr or Upwork.** For **premium, custom designs, 99designs or Reedsy** are better options.

Common Book Cover Mistakes to Avoid

Even experienced designers can make mistakes. Here are some common pitfalls:

- **Unreadable Text:** Ensure that your title and author name are **clear and legible,** even at smaller sizes.
- **Overcrowding:** Too many elements **clutter the design.** Stick to key visuals and **maintain a balanced composition.**
- **Generic Imagery:** Avoid **overused stock images** that don't make your book stand out.
- **Ignoring Branding:** Your cover should reflect the **tone, style, and audience** of your book. Consistency matters, especially for a book series.

Next Steps

Your **book cover is your most powerful marketing tool.** Whether you choose to design it yourself using **free or paid** tools, or **hire a professional**, the key is to **make sure your cover speaks to your audience and represents your book well.**

Before finalizing your cover, consider **testing different designs** with potential readers. **A/B testing** through social media polls or reader communities can provide valuable feedback and help you choose the most effective design.

A **well-designed cover** attracts readers, increases visibility, and contributes to **your overall success as an author.**

In the next chapter, we'll dive into the **final steps of uploading your manuscript and cover to KDP**, ensuring everything is properly set up for publication.

8. Publishing Your Book on KDP

Getting Ready to Go Live

Publishing on KDP is the moment when your book transitions from an idea to a product available to readers worldwide. Understanding the process ensures that your book is not only live but also positioned for success. In this chapter, we'll walk you through the detailed process of uploading your book to KDP, setting up your book's listing, and optimizing it for discoverability.

> *"The beautiful part of writing is that you don't have to get it right the first time. The most important thing is to finish, then publish."*
>
> *— Shannon Hale*

SETTING UP YOUR KDP ACCOUNT

Before you can publish your book on KDP, you'll need to set up an account. If you haven't done this already, follow these steps:

- **Sign Up:** Go to the <u>KDP homepage</u> and sign in with your Amazon account. If you don't have one, you'll need to create it.
- **Tax & Payment Information:** Enter your tax details (for royalties) and payment preferences to ensure you receive earnings from your book sales. This step is required before publishing.
- **Set Up Your Author Profile:** Adding an author photo and biography helps build credibility and encourages readers to explore your other works.

CREATING YOUR NEW BOOK

Once your KDP account is set up, you can start the process of publishing your book. KDP provides an intuitive step-by-step guide, which includes:

Book Details & Metadata

On the first page, you'll enter key details about your book. This step directly impacts how your book is displayed, categorized, and discovered on Amazon.

- **Book Title & Subtitle:** Ensure your title is compelling and clear. A well-crafted subtitle can add value and context.
- **Author Name & Contributors:** Enter your name (or pen name) and list any contributors (e.g., editors, illustrators).
- **Rights & Territories:** Select where you hold distribution

rights. Most authors choose **Worldwide Rights** unless specific regional restrictions apply.

- **Book Description:** This serves as your sales pitch. It should be engaging, persuasive, and keyword-rich to attract potential readers. The first few lines are crucial, as Amazon only displays a preview before the "Read More" button.
- **Keywords:** Choose up to **seven keywords** that best describe your book. These keywords influence Amazon's search algorithm and help readers find your book. Research keyword trends using **Publisher Rocket** or **Google Keyword Planner**.
- **Categories:** Select three categories that best fit your book. Choosing **niche categories** (see Chapter 2) can improve discoverability and ranking potential.
- **Series Information:** If your book is part of a series, include the series name and volume number.

KDP Select and Kindle Unlimited

Enrolling in **KDP Select** makes your eBook exclusive to Amazon for **90 days** and allows it to be included in **Kindle Unlimited (KU)**, Amazon's subscription service. Readers can borrow your book at no extra cost, and you earn royalties based on **pages read**.

Pros:

- Access to Kindle Unlimited's large subscriber base.
- Promotional tools like **Kindle Countdown Deals** and the ability to offer free promotions.
- Higher visibility in Amazon's search rankings.

Cons:

- Exclusivity to Amazon—your book cannot be sold on Apple Books, Barnes & Noble, or Google Play during the 90-day period.
- If you later decide to publish on other platforms, you'll need to **wait until your 90-day exclusivity period expires** before opting out.

If you want broader distribution, you may opt **not** to enroll in KDP Select and instead publish through platforms like **IngramSpark, Draft2Digital, or Smashwords** (more on this in the next chapter).

Uploading Your Content & Previewing

This step involves uploading your **manuscript** and **cover**, followed by previewing your book.

Manuscript Upload

KDP accepts:

- **DOCX** – Best for simple uploads with automated conversion.
- **EPUB** – Ideal for maintaining custom formatting.
- **KPF (Kindle Create File)** – Optimized format for books created using Kindle Create.

Cover Upload

- **eBook Covers:** Upload a **JPEG or TIFF** file.
- **Print Covers:** Upload a **PDF** with embedded fonts.
- **Use KDP's Cover Creator** if you don't have a professionally designed cover.

Preview Tool

Before publishing, use the **KDP Previewer** to check formatting across different devices (Kindle eReaders, tablets, and apps). Ensure that:

- Page breaks and spacing are correct.
- Fonts and text alignment display properly.
- Images and graphics appear as intended.

If any issues arise, fix them and re-upload your files before moving forward.

Pricing & Royalties

Once your content is uploaded, you'll set your **pricing and royalty structure.**

Royalty Options

- **35% Royalty:** Available if your eBook is priced below **$2.99** or above **$9.99**, or if you choose not to enroll in KDP Select.
- **70% Royalty:** Available for eBooks priced between **$2.99** and **$9.99** and distributed in eligible territories.
- **Print Books:** KDP offers a **60% royalty** for paperbacks, minus **printing costs**, which vary by page count and ink type.

Distribution Options

- **Enroll in Kindle Unlimited (KU)** to gain visibility with subscribers.
- **Sell Directly on Amazon** without KU exclusivity, allowing you to distribute through other platforms.
- **International Pricing:** You can set country-specific

pricing or let Amazon adjust automatically based on exchange rates.

It's a good idea to experiment with pricing. Many authors find that adjusting their price over time helps them find the sweet spot for maximizing sales and royalties.

Once you finalize pricing and distribution, **click "Publish"** to submit your book for review. Amazon typically approves books within **24-72 hours.**

OPTIMIZING FOR MAXIMUM PROFIT

Pricing strategy plays a **critical role** in maximizing your earnings. Experiment with different price points and promotions to see what resonates with your audience. This will be discussed in detail later in the book. However, consider:

- **Limited-time discounts** to boost initial sales and rankings.
- **Regular price adjustments** to stay competitive in your genre.
- **Using Amazon Ads** to increase visibility and drive traffic.

OTHER PUBLISHING PLATFORMS

While KDP is Amazon's primary self-publishing platform, you may want to explore other distribution channels like:

- **IngramSpark** – Ideal for wide print book distribution.
- **Draft2Digital** – Distributes to Apple Books, Barnes & Noble, and Kobo.
- **PublishDrive** – Similar to Draft2Digital but adds Google Play Books amid a vast network of others offering wider international distribution.

If your eBook is in **Kindle Unlimited (KDP Select)**, you **cannot** publish it on these platforms until the **90-day exclusivity period** ends. More on this in the next chapter.

Next Steps

By now, your book is ready for launch! After completing the upload, content, and pricing sections, simply **click "Publish"** to submit your book for review. Once Amazon approves it, your book will be live and available for sale within **24-72 hours**.

With your book now published, the real challenge begins—getting readers to find and buy it. In the next chapter, we'll dive into proven marketing strategies to boost visibility, increase sales, and establish your presence as an author.

9. Pricing & Royalties – How to Maximize Profit

Setting the Right Price

Pricing isn't just about setting a number—it's about understanding **reader psychology, market expectations, and maximizing revenue potential**. The right price can make the difference between steady sales and stagnation. Let's explore the key strategies for setting the best price.

> *"Royalties are like a slow leak in a bucket—at first, they seem small, but over time, they can fill a well."*

— Hugh Howey

Case Study: Maximizing Revenue Through Price Adjustments

Michael released his self-published business book at $0.99 to attract early reviews. After gaining traction, he gradually increased the price to $4.99. His royalties tripled while maintaining strong sales volume.

Key Takeaways:

- Start low for visibility, then adjust pricing once the book has social proof.
- Pricing experimentation can significantly impact revenue.

Understanding KDP's Pricing Models

KDP provides two main royalty options for eBooks and a fixed royalty model for print books:

eBooks:

- **35% Royalty Option:** Applies if your eBook is priced **below $2.99 or above $9.99**, or if you choose **not** to enroll in KDP Select.
- **70% Royalty Option:** Available for eBooks priced **between $2.99 and $9.99**, provided the book is enrolled in KDP Select (Amazon exclusivity required).

Print Books:

- The royalty rate is **60% of the list price, minus printing costs**. Printing costs vary based on **page count, ink type, and format.**

Choosing Your Price Point

When setting your price, consider the following factors:

- **Genre Expectations:** Certain genres have pricing norms. Romance novels often range between **$2.99 and $4.99**, while non-fiction books with niche expertise can justify **higher prices ($5.99–$14.99)**.
- **Length and Value:** Shorter books (under **50 pages**) are typically priced at **$0.99–$2.99**, while full-length books can command **$5.99–$9.99** or more.
- **Competitor Pricing:** Research similar books in your genre to identify pricing trends. Here's how to conduct a competitor analysis:
    1. Search for books in your genre on Amazon.
    2. Note the **price ranges** of top-selling books.
    3. Read reviews to understand **reader expectations**.
    4. Track whether books **change pricing over time**, especially during promotions.

PRICE TESTING & ADJUSTMENTS

Your book's **best price is not fixed**—testing different price points can reveal the optimal balance between volume and profit.

Strategies for Price Testing:

- **Experiment with price points:** Try pricing at **$4.99 for a few weeks**, then adjust to **$3.99 or $5.99** and monitor sales trends. For example, if sales stagnate at **$4.99**, lowering it to **$3.99** may increase volume. Conversely, if demand is strong, raising it to **$5.99** could boost overall revenue.
- **Use KDP Reports:** Leverage Amazon's **Sales Dashboard and Book Report tools** to track the impact of price changes.
- **Apply Promotional Pricing:** Utilize **Kindle Countdown Deals** or **free promotions** (if enrolled in KDP Select) to drive visibility and attract new readers.

Royalties in Different Markets

Amazon allows you to **set custom pricing** for each international market, optimizing your book's appeal across regions.

- **Global Reach:** Consider **adjusting prices** for economies with different purchasing power. For example, a **$9.99** book may be too expensive in India, where a lower price point can increase sales.
- **Currency & Exchange Rates:** Amazon automatically converts your pricing, but **manual price adjustments** ensure competitive pricing per region.

The Impact of KDP Select on Pricing and Royalties

KDP Select offers exclusive promotional tools but **requires your eBook to remain exclusive to Amazon for 90 days.**

Key Benefits:

- **Kindle Unlimited (KU):** Books in KU earn royalties based on **pages read,** which can **outperform direct sales** if your book is widely read.
- **Promotional Tools:** Offers **Kindle Countdown Deals** and **Free Promotions** to increase visibility.
- **Higher Amazon Visibility:** KDP Select books often receive **better ranking boosts** within Amazon's search algorithm.

Potential Drawbacks:

- **Amazon Exclusivity:** You **cannot** sell your eBook on **Apple Books, Barnes & Noble, or Kobo** while enrolled.

- **Market Limitations:** KU is beneficial for **frequent readers,** but if your audience prefers to purchase books outright, wide distribution may be better.
- **Print Book Sales Are Unaffected:** Unlike eBooks, print books **can still be distributed through IngramSpark and other print-on-demand services** even if your eBook is in KDP Select.

If you choose KDP Select but later want to go wide, **opt out before the 90-day renewal** to regain distribution flexibility.

OTHER PUBLISHING & DISTRIBUTION PLATFORMS

While KDP is Amazon's primary self-publishing platform, you may want to explore other distribution channels to expand your reach. Depending on your goals, you can publish directly on major platforms or use an aggregator for broader distribution.

Direct Publishing Options:

- **Google Play Books** – A growing platform with global reach, offering flexible pricing and promotional tools.
- **Apple Books** – Ideal for reaching Apple device users and growing an audience outside Amazon.
- **Kobo Writing Life** – Strong in international markets, especially in Canada, Europe, and Australia.
- **Barnes & Noble Press** – A solid choice for direct publishing to Nook readers in the U.S.

Aggregator Platforms:

If managing multiple platforms individually is time-consuming, aggregators can streamline distribution across multiple retailers.

- **IngramSpark** – Best for wide print book distribution to bookstores, libraries, and online retailers.
- **Draft2Digital** – Distributes eBooks to Apple Books, Barnes & Noble, Kobo, and other major retailers with a user-friendly interface.
- **PublishDrive** – Offers global eBook, audiobook, and print distribution with royalty optimization features.

When to Use an Aggregator vs. Direct Publishing:

- **Go Direct If:** You want **higher royalties**, better platform control, and access to platform-specific promotions (e.g., Kobo promotions, Google Play discounts).
- **Use an Aggregator If:** You want **convenience, one dashboard to manage all platforms, and wider international distribution.**

Important: If your eBook is enrolled in **Kindle Unlimited (KDP Select)**, you **cannot** publish it on other platforms until the **90-day exclusivity period ends.**

NEXT STEPS

Pricing is only one part of the equation—marketing is what ensures your book actually sells. By now, you should have a solid understanding of **pricing strategies, royalties, and KDP Select considerations.** Be prepared to **test, adjust, and optimize** based on reader demand and sales data.

Choosing the right price for your book is not just about maximizing royalties—it's also a key factor in your **overall marketing strategy.** A well-priced book is easier to promote, more likely to attract readers, and can generate **sustained sales momentum.** But pricing alone isn't enough. To drive consistent book sales, you need a **strategic marketing approach** that puts your book in front of the right audience at the right time. In the next chapter, we'll dive into marketing strategies that will help you generate visibility, attract readers, and turn your book into **a sustainable source of income.**

10. Marketing & Generating Sales

Why Marketing Matters

Publishing your book is just the beginning. Without effective marketing, even the best-written book may go unnoticed. Marketing is not about 'selling'—it's about **connecting your book with the right readers.** The strategies in this chapter will help you generate sales, build an audience, and create a **sustainable author career.**

Many authors struggle with marketing because they **feel overwhelmed** by the options or don't know where to start. This chapter simplifies the process, giving you **clear strategies** to attract readers and **generate consistent sales.**

Marketing is what gets your book in front of potential readers, builds your author brand, and ultimately **generates sales.** A strong marketing plan can mean the difference between a book that sells a few copies and one that creates a steady stream of income. In this chapter, we'll explore both free and paid marketing strategies, real-world examples, cost estimates, and reasons why certain approaches work better than others.

. . .

"Writing the book is only half the battle. The other half is letting the world know it exists."

— *Jodi Picoult*

BUILDING A STRONG FOUNDATION BEFORE LAUNCH

Before you publish your book, take a moment to strategize. A well-prepared launch can make all the difference in gaining early traction. Think of it like opening a new restaurant—you wouldn't just put up a sign and hope people walk in. You'd **advertise, invite food critics, and ensure everything is perfect before opening night.**

Author Website & Social Media Presence

Even if you're not tech-savvy, having a basic online presence is crucial. Your website serves as your **virtual home base.** It doesn't have to be fancy—a simple one-page author website with **links to your books, an author bio, and a contact form** is a great start. Platforms like **Wix, Squarespace, and WordPress** offer easy drag-and-drop templates.

Instead of trying to be everywhere, focus on **1-2 platforms** where your readers are most active. Use content marketing—**behind-the-scenes insights, writing tips, or themed posts**—to attract engagement without feeling overly promotional.

Many authors have found success by leveraging **BookTok on TikTok**—posting short, engaging clips about their books. Others use **Substack or Medium** to create blog posts related to their niche, driving organic traffic to their books.

Email List & Lead Magnets

Your email list is the only audience you truly own—unlike social media followers, who are at the mercy of ever-changing algorithms.

Start building your list by offering a freebie (a **"lead magnet"**) in exchange for emails. This could be a **sample chapter, exclusive short story, or a helpful guide** related to your book's topic. Platforms like **Mailchimp, Kit, and SendFox** make it easy to manage your list and send updates.

One successful case study involves an author who offered a **companion workbook** for their non-fiction book. This not only helped build an email list but also created a built-in audience for future book releases.

Amazon Author Central Page

Your **Amazon Author Central** profile is like your **digital storefront**. Add a **professional bio, a high-quality author photo, and links to your books**. Readers can "follow" you on Amazon and get notified when you release a new book. If you have editorial reviews, blog posts, or even videos, add them here for extra credibility.

LEVERAGING AMAZON'S INTERNAL MARKETING TOOLS

Amazon rewards books that perform well, so using its built-in tools effectively can increase your visibility. Many new authors underestimate how powerful Amazon's internal algorithms are. If your book is **well-optimized**, Amazon will do some of the marketing for you.

Amazon SEO: Keywords & Categories

Choosing the right **keywords and categories** is one of the easiest ways to improve discoverability. The right category selection can make your book a **#1 bestseller in a niche genre**, giving it a **permanent boost** in visibility.

Tools like **Publisher Rocket** help you find **keywords that real Amazon shoppers are searching for.** Other keyword research tools include **KDSpy** (one-time payment of $69), **Helium 10** (subscription-based, starting at $39/month), and **KDP Champ** (monthly plans for advanced tracking and analytics). These tools provide valuable insights into Amazon search trends, competition analysis, and category selection, helping authors optimize their book listings for better discoverability.

Another simple trick is typing potential book topics into the **Amazon search bar** and noting the autocomplete suggestions— these are **actual terms people use when searching for books.**

For example, if you're publishing a self-help book on productivity, instead of just using 'productivity' as a keyword, consider long-tail keywords like '**time management for busy professionals**' or '**productivity tips for remote workers**' to capture more specific searches.

FREE & ORGANIC MARKETING STRATEGIES

If you're on a tight budget, don't worry—there are plenty of ways to promote your book without spending a dime.

Leveraging Book Bloggers & Influencers

Instead of cold-emailing big names, start small. Connect with potential reviewers through platforms like **Goodreads, Bookstagram (Instagram for book lovers), X (Twitter) writing communities, and Facebook book groups.**

Websites like **The IndieView and Reedsy Discovery** list book bloggers open to reviewing self-published books. Offer them a free review copy and make it **easy for them to say yes** by providing a **short, compelling pitch** about your book and why it fits their audience.

One author grew their email list to **5,000 subscribers** by posting **serialized stories on Medium and Substack,** which funneled readers to their published books.

PAID MARKETING STRATEGIES

Amazon Ads vs. Facebook Ads vs. BookBub Ads

Each platform has unique advantages, and choosing the right one depends on your book's **genre, goals, and budget.**

Amazon Ads – Best for **direct sales** on Amazon.

- Recommended Budget: **$5–$50 per day (see below)**
- Pros: High-intent audience, integrates directly with Kindle store rankings
- Cons: Requires ongoing testing and budget adjustments
- For authors looking to increase Amazon store visibility and organic ranking

Facebook Ads – Best for **building an audience and retargeting.**

- Recommended Budget: **$10–$50 per day**
- Pros: Highly customizable targeting, great for lead generation and branding
- Cons: Conversion rates can vary, may require multiple touchpoints to turn a click into a sale
- For authors who want to build an audience before launch or retarget past customers

BookBub Ads – Best for **promotions, discounts, and new releases.**

- Recommended Budget: **$100–$500 per campaign**

- Pros: Strong conversion rates, direct access to readers who actively purchase books
- Cons: Can be expensive and highly competitive
- Best for authors running promotions, launching a new book, or increasing exposure in specific genres

Pro Tip: Use **Facebook Ads** to **build an email list** before launch, then switch to **Amazon Ads** to **boost rankings** upon release.

If you're new to ads, start with a **low daily budget ($5–$10/day)** on **Amazon Ads** with **automatic targeting**. Once you identify effective keywords, shift to manual targeting and increase your budget based on performance:

- Paid marketing strategies need updates based on **rising Amazon CPC costs.**
- **Recommended budget:** Adjusted to **$10–$75 per day** for competitive keywords and proper ad optimization.
- **ACoS (Advertising Cost of Sales) awareness:** ACoS represents the percentage of your ad spend compared to book sales generated from those ads. Ideally, you should aim for an ACoS **below 70%** to break even, but profitability varies by book price and niche. A healthy target for sustained profit is **under 50%**, meaning you're earning more from sales than you're spending on ads. Additionally, tracking **Total ACoS (TACoS)** helps determine if ads are driving overall sales, including organic purchases not directly attributed to ad clicks. Lowering ACoS over time while increasing TACoS indicates that ads are boosting long-term book visibility and sales beyond paid clicks.
- **Manual targeting best practices:** Once effective keywords are found in **auto campaigns**, shift to manual bidding to lower costs.

GETTING BOOK REVIEWS & SOCIAL PROOF

Reviews are a **critical part** of your book's success. Amazon's algorithm **favors books with strong review numbers,** and potential readers often check reviews before making a purchase.

How to Get More Reviews (Ethically)

- **Give away Advance Reader Copies (ARCs)** to early readers.
- **Engage with book clubs** that align with your genre.
- **Use platforms like NetGalley** to connect with reviewers.
- **Encourage readers** via your email list and website.

Pro Tip: Reach out to engaged readers from your **email list or social media** and offer an **ARC (Advance Reader Copy)** in exchange for an honest review. **Personal requests** are more effective than mass outreach.

Review Request Template: *"Hi [Reader's Name], I hope you're enjoying [Book Title]! If you found it helpful or entertaining, I'd love it if you could leave a quick review on Amazon. Your feedback helps other readers decide if the book is right for them. Here's the link: [Insert Link]. Thanks so much for your support!"*

LONG-TERM MARKETING STRATEGY

A single marketing push **isn't enough.** Authors who build sustainable careers use strategies like:

- **Retargeting past buyers** (Amazon & Facebook allow retargeting ads).
- **Creating seasonal promotions** (discounting books during holidays).

- **Automating campaigns** (using AI-driven ad management tools).
- **Reinvesting earnings** into advertising for continuous growth.

NEXT STEPS: SUSTAINABLE SUCCESS IN MARKETING

Marketing is an **ongoing process,** not a one-time push. The best-selling authors **test, refine, and adapt** their strategies. As you continue to publish, your marketing skills will evolve, making each new book launch **smoother and more successful.**

Once you've implemented a solid marketing strategy, your book will begin generating sales. But how do you turn that initial success into a sustainable publishing business? The most successful authors don't rely on a single book or marketing campaign—they expand into multiple revenue streams, formats, and markets. In the next chapter, we'll explore **how to scale your publishing business beyond KDP,** including **audiobooks, translations, and other income streams.**

11. Scaling Your Publishing Business

Embracing the Growth Mindset

Publishing a book is a significant accomplishment, but if you want to build a sustainable career, you need to **think beyond a single release.** Scaling your publishing business means expanding your offerings, maximizing efficiency, and **leveraging new opportunities** to create multiple income streams. This isn't about working harder—**it's about working smarter** and making your books work for you.

While scaling a publishing business is exciting, many authors face challenges such as **burnout, inconsistent revenue, or difficulty managing multiple projects.** This chapter provides solutions to these common hurdles, helping you scale efficiently without losing momentum. Whether you aim to be a full-time author or simply want to increase your book sales, this chapter will explore strategies to grow your publishing business effectively.

"Scaling your business means creating systems and structures that allow you to replicate your success without losing quality or passion."

— *Tim Ferriss*

Case Study: From Book to Course Sales

Derek published a book on real estate investing and included a link to a free guide. His email list grew, and he launched an online course for $297. Within six months, course sales surpassed book royalties tenfold.

Key Takeaways:

- Books can act as lead magnets for higher-ticket products.
- A structured funnel increases lifetime customer value.

Expanding Your Offerings: Sourcing & Repurposing Content

Not all books need to start from scratch. Many successful authors leverage existing content to create new products. Here's how you can do the same:

Repurpose Content from Blogs, Podcasts, and Courses

- Compile blog posts into a book with additional insights and refinements.
- Edit podcast transcripts into a structured book format to reach audiences who prefer reading over listening.
- Adapt online courses or workshop materials into step-by-step guides, workbooks, or industry insights.

Example: An entrepreneur who ran a successful blog about personal finance compiled his most popular posts into a well-structured book, added case studies, and launched it as a bestseller in the budgeting category.

Public Domain Publishing

- Republish classic works in the public domain with added commentary, modernized language, or annotations.
- Curate collections of thematically relevant works and create annotated guides or study editions.

Low-Content Publishing

- Create and sell journals, planners, and workbooks that align with your brand or niche.
- Use tools like **BookBolt** and **Tangent Templates** to automate the design process for low-content books.

By leveraging existing content and tapping into underutilized publishing opportunities, you can quickly expand your catalog and reach more readers without starting from zero.

ENHANCING WRITING EFFICIENCY & INCREASING PRODUCTIVITY

If you want to publish more books without sacrificing quality, you need systems in place to streamline your workflow and improve your writing habits.

Develop a Writing Routine

- Set a realistic daily or weekly word count goal and stick to it.

- Use the **Pomodoro technique** (writing in focused 25-minute sprints) to improve concentration.
- Speed up drafting with dictation software like **Dragon NaturallySpeaking** or **Google Voice Typing**.

Using AI & Automation

- AI tools like **Sudowrite, ChatGPT, or Claude AI** can assist with outlining, brainstorming, and generating first drafts.
- Automate research with AI-assisted summarization tools to quickly gather insights on a topic.

Batching Tasks & Optimizing Workflow

- Write multiple books in the same series or niche simultaneously to maintain consistency and speed up production.
- Outsource repetitive tasks (editing, formatting, cover design) to freelancers via platforms like **Reedsy, Fiverr, and Upwork.**
- Pre-plan book marketing and launch strategies in bulk so they run automatically when a new book is released.

By focusing on efficiency, automation, and structured workflows, you can increase your output without feeling overwhelmed.

Expanding into Different Formats

Once you have books published, you can multiply their value by offering them in different formats:

Audiobooks:

- Use platforms like **ACX (Audible), Findaway Voices, or Speechki** to convert books into audiobooks.
- Choose between hiring a professional narrator or using AI-generated voice narration.

Hardcover & Large Print Editions:

- Offer **premium hardcover versions** for collectors or libraries.
- Create **large print editions** for visually impaired readers and older audiences.

Translations & Foreign Markets:

- Expand into new markets by translating books into **Spanish, German, French**, and other widely spoken languages.
- Work with **Babelcube, human translators, or AI-assisted translation services.**
- Leverage **regional marketing strategies** to gain traction in international markets.

By optimizing your book's availability in multiple formats, you increase discoverability and open up additional revenue streams with minimal extra work.

ADDITIONAL REVENUE STREAMS

Beyond book sales, there are multiple ways to monetize your expertise and brand. Here are some proven strategies:

Direct Sales via Website

- Sell books directly through platforms like **Shopify, Gumroad, or Payhip.**

- Offer bundled deals (e.g., signed copies, book + workbook sets).

Crowdfunding & Subscription Models

- Use **Kickstarter** to fund your next book launch.
- Offer exclusive content on **Patreon or Ream** for readers who support you monthly.

Online Courses & Workshops

- Convert your book's content into an **online course** hosted on **Teachable or Udemy**.
- Offer **live workshops or coaching** related to your book's niche.

Affiliate Marketing & Brand Collaborations

- Promote tools, books, or software related to your niche and **earn commissions.**
- Partner with brands to **cross-promote products** relevant to your audience.

By diversifying income streams, you reduce reliance on a single revenue source and create financial stability as an author.

THE BUSINESS ASPECTS OF PUBLISHING

Once your publishing business starts growing, it's essential to handle the legal and operational aspects professionally.

Intellectual Property & Licensing

- License your **book rights** to foreign publishers for additional revenue.

- Explore **film, TV, or game adaptation** opportunities.
- Secure **trademarks** for your series titles and brand identity.
- **KDP ISBN Limitations:** If an author uses a **KDP-assigned ISBN**, they **can only distribute print books through Amazon** and cannot use *that ISBN* for wide distribution (e.g., IngramSpark, bookstores, or libraries). Authors who wish to distribute widely should purchase their own ISBN—**in the US through Bowker (MyIdentifiers.com), in the UK through Nielsen, and in Canada through Library and Archives Canada, where ISBNs are available for free.**

Print-on-Demand vs. Bulk Printing

- Use **POD (Print-on-Demand)** for low-risk printing with services like **KDP Print and IngramSpark.**
- Consider **bulk printing** and distribution if you have a large, engaged audience.
- *Break-even point:* Bulk printing is cost-effective when ordering **500+ copies,** but POD is better for lower-risk inventory management.
- *Storage considerations:* Bulk orders require **warehousing or fulfillment solutions** if selling direct.

Setting Up a Business Entity

- Register an **LLC or S-Corp** for tax benefits and liability protection.
- LLC provides **liability protection and flexible tax options.**
- S-Corp allows for **lower self-employment taxes** if your business reaches a certain revenue level.

- Track **expenses and earnings** with bookkeeping software like **QuickBooks or Wave**.

Understanding the business side of publishing ensures you maximize profits while protecting your assets.

NEXT STEPS: SUSTAINABLE GROWTH STRATEGIES

Scaling your publishing business requires **strategy, efficiency, and diversification.** By repurposing content, increasing productivity, expanding into different formats, and establishing additional revenue streams, you create a sustainable model that grows over time.

However, **growth comes with its own set of challenges.** Many authors struggle with **burnout, financial setbacks, or spreading themselves too thin.** Knowing how to **identify and avoid common pitfalls** will ensure that your publishing business remains profitable and manageable in the long run.

In the next chapter, we'll explore the most frequent obstacles authors face while scaling and how to navigate them successfully —so you can **continue growing your publishing business without unnecessary setbacks.**

12. Overcoming Challenges & Avoiding Common Pitfalls

Why Challenges Are Inevitable in Publishing

Self-publishing isn't a straight path to success. Many new authors believe that once they've written a book, the rest will take care of itself—but reality is much different. Even experienced authors face setbacks, whether in writing, marketing, or managing the business side of publishing.

> *"Publishing is a tough business. If you want to succeed, you have to keep pushing, even when the odds seem against you."*
>
> — *Margaret Atwood*

The good news? Every challenge is an opportunity to refine your approach and grow. Fortunately, by recognizing these pitfalls early and applying practical solutions, you can avoid unnecessary setbacks and build a sustainable publishing business. The key is recognizing common pitfalls, preparing for them, and having the right strategies in place to adapt and thrive. This chapter will walk you through the most frequent mistakes self-published authors make and how to avoid them.

CASE STUDY: RELAUNCHING A FAILED BOOK

Mark's first book flopped due to poor editing. Negative reviews tanked his ranking. He hired an editor, republished, and rebranded the book. Within six months, his relaunch brought in $2,000/month.

Key Takeaways:

- Editing and presentation matter—bad reviews can kill a book.
- Relaunching can salvage an underperforming title.

WRITING & PRODUCTIVITY PITFALLS

Overcoming Writer's Block & Perfectionism

It's easy to get stuck, staring at a blank screen, waiting for the perfect words. Many authors never finish their first book because they overthink every sentence.

How to Overcome It:

- **Set Realistic Deadlines** – A book will never be perfect— set a firm finish date and move on.
- **Use the Pomodoro Technique** – Write in 25-minute focused sprints with short breaks to maintain momentum.
- **Outline First** – A clear roadmap prevents you from getting lost in the middle of your book.
- **Leverage AI & Dictation** – Use tools like **Sudowrite, ChatGPT, or Dragon NaturallySpeaking** to draft ideas quickly.

Burnout & Fatigue from Overproduction

Some authors push themselves to write as fast as possible, only to burn out before they can enjoy the success of their books.

Avoiding Burnout:

- **Pace Yourself** – A sustainable writing pace could be one book every 3–6 months, depending on complexity, audience demand, and personal capacity.
- **Batch Work** – Write in phases—first drafts, edits, and marketing should have distinct focus periods.
- **Outsource Where Possible** – If formatting, editing, or marketing drain your time, hire freelancers to handle them.

BOOK QUALITY & COMMON FORMATTING ERRORS

Why First Impressions Matter

Readers judge books by their covers—and their formatting. Sloppy presentation leads to bad reviews, which can kill your book before it gains traction.

How to Ensure Professional Quality:

- **Invest in a Good Cover** – DIY covers rarely work. Hire a professional designer on **Reedsy, Fiverr, or 99designs.**
- **Avoid Formatting Errors** – Poorly formatted books frustrate readers and hurt reviews.
  - Use **Vellum (Mac) or Atticus (PC & Mac)** for clean, professional formatting.
  - Hire a formatter if you're publishing print books via **IngramSpark.**
- **Get Beta Readers & Editors** – Fresh eyes catch mistakes you'll miss.

○ **Developmental editors** refine structure, while **proofreaders** ensure the final polish.

MARKETING & SALES PITFALLS

Misunderstanding Book Marketing

One of the biggest myths in self-publishing is that simply uploading your book will lead to sales. Marketing is not optional.

What Works:

- **Targeted Ads** – Amazon Ads and Facebook Ads should be carefully tested before scaling up.
- **Email Marketing Is Crucial** – Your email list is your best long-term asset.
- **Leverage Reviews & Influencers** – Outreach to book bloggers, TikTok reviewers, and ARC readers.

Poor Keyword & Category Selection on Amazon

Amazon is a search engine. If you pick the wrong keywords, your book will be buried.

How to Choose the Right Keywords & Categories:

- Use **Publisher Rocket or KDSpy** to find low-competition, high-search-volume keywords.
- Choose **niche categories** where your book can rank as a bestseller.
- Avoid misleading categories—choosing the wrong niche leads to poor reader experiences and low retention.

Running Ineffective Ads & Wasting Money

Many authors dive into paid advertising without a clear strategy, spending hundreds with no results. Monitor click-through rates and conversion data to adjust your strategy rather than blindly increasing your ad spend.

How to Optimize Ads:

- **Start Small** – Test Amazon or Facebook Ads with $5–$10/day before committing a large budget.
- **Analyze & Adjust** – If your ad isn't converting, check your cover, blurb, and pricing before scaling up.
- **Use Amazon Ads for Visibility** – Even with a low budget, Amazon Ads boost organic sales ranking.

BUILDING LONG-TERM READER ENGAGEMENT & COMMUNITY

While marketing brings in new readers, long-term success in publishing relies on building a loyal audience.

The Importance of Reader Engagement

- Engaged readers are more likely to leave reviews, recommend books, and buy future releases.
- Building a community creates a support network that drives organic sales and word-of-mouth promotion.

Ways to Build Reader Loyalty:

- **Email Newsletters** – Offer free content, behind-the-scenes updates, and personal insights.
- **Exclusive Reader Groups** – Host a **Facebook group or Discord community** for fans to interact.
- **Interactive Content** – Run **Q&A sessions, live readings, and contests** to keep readers engaged.

Over-Reliance on One Platform & Business Risk

Amazon Exclusivity (KDP Select) Pros & Cons

Pros:

- Higher royalties in certain territories.
- Additional income from Kindle Unlimited pages read.
- Access to Kindle Countdown Deals and Free Promotions.

Cons:

- No wide distribution (Apple Books, Kobo, Google Play).
- Limited pricing control.
- Dependency on Amazon's algorithm, which can change unexpectedly.

Diversify by:

- **Going Wide** – Publish on **Apple Books, Kobo, Google Play, and Barnes & Noble.**
- **Selling Direct** – Use platforms like **Gumroad, Payhip, or Shopify.**
- **Building an Email List** – So your audience follows you, not just Amazon's algorithm.

Scaling Too Quickly Without a Plan

Some authors try to release too many books too fast or invest heavily in ads before securing steady income. A more sustainable approach is to focus on a strong backlist before scaling.

Sustainable Scaling Strategies:

- **Build a Backlist First** – Having multiple books increases income stability.
- **Automate Repetitive Tasks** – Use tools to handle email sequences, book formatting, and ad tracking.
- **Scale Smartly** – Only expand once you have steady monthly income.

ADDITIONAL READING & RESOURCES

For further study on these challenges, consider:

- *Write. Publish. Repeat.* by Sean Platt & Johnny B. Truant – A practical guide to long-term success in self-publishing.
- *Let's Get Digital* by David Gaughran – Covers marketing strategies for indie authors.
- *The 10X Author* by Sean M. Sumner – Focuses on rapid book production without burnout.
- Kindlepreneur Blog (kindlepreneur.com) – Free articles on keyword research, Amazon algorithms, and book marketing.
- Self-Publishing Podcast by Mark Dawson – Covers advanced marketing, advertising, and book launch strategies.

NEXT STEPS: TURNING CHALLENGES INTO GROWTH OPPORTUNITIES

Every successful author has faced failures—what matters is how you adapt and learn. Mistakes are part of the journey, but by avoiding these common pitfalls, you'll set yourself up for long-term success.

The next step is developing strategies to ensure sustainable growth. In the next chapter, we'll explore advanced methods for maintaining long-term success in the publishing industry.

13. Long-Term Strategies & Building a Sustainable Publishing Business

The Shift from Author to Publisher

Publishing a book is a major milestone, but long-term success requires more than simply writing and releasing more books. To build a sustainable publishing business, you must shift from thinking like an author to acting like a publisher—one who strategically expands their reach, diversifies income streams, and builds systems that ensure longevity in the industry.

This chapter moves beyond short-term tactics and focuses on the strategies that help authors develop a lasting and profitable publishing business.

"In the writing and publishing world, long-term success is a product of passion, persistence, and the ability to adapt."

— *Joanna Penn*

Case Study: Licensing Books for Passive Income

Emma, a career coach, licensed her book to corporations for training programs. Instead of earning only from Amazon royalties, she secured deals paying **$5,000 per company per year.**

Key Takeaways:

- Licensing can generate long-term, passive income.
- Businesses value well-structured educational content.

Creating a Scalable Publishing Model

Many authors fall into the cycle of constantly writing new books without optimizing their existing catalog. A sustainable publishing business is built on long-term planning and systemization rather than chasing short-term sales.

Key Steps for Scaling:

- **Build a Long-Term Catalog Strategy** – Instead of releasing books one at a time, develop a multi-book plan that includes sequels, companion books, or spin-offs.
- **Optimize Backlist Performance** – Ensure that older books remain relevant by refreshing covers, updating metadata, and leveraging seasonal promotions.
- **Create Evergreen Content** – Books with lasting relevance continue to generate revenue without relying on trends.

Rather than focusing solely on new releases, successful authors maximize what they already have, ensuring consistent income without burnout.

Structuring a Publishing Business for Efficiency

Once multiple books are published, managing releases, marketing, and finances can become overwhelming. A structured business approach helps maintain consistency and growth.

Core Business Foundations:

- **Register a Business Entity** – Whether an LLC or sole proprietorship, formalizing the business protects assets and streamlines tax management.
- **Implement a Production Pipeline** – Develop a repeatable workflow for writing, editing, formatting, and launching books.
- **Leverage Automation & AI** – Use tools like Notion, Trello, or AI-driven content generators to manage tasks efficiently.
- **Outsource Strategically** – Focus on writing and high-level strategy while delegating editing, formatting, and design to professionals.

A structured approach prevents bottlenecks and ensures a publishing business runs efficiently as it grows.

Diversifying Income Beyond Amazon Royalties

Relying solely on book sales through Amazon limits financial security. Expanding into alternative revenue sources creates resilience against industry shifts.

Monetization Strategies to Expand Revenue:

- **Direct Sales via Author Website** – Selling books directly through platforms like Shopify or Payhip increases profits per sale.

- **Subscription-Based Content** – Platforms like Ream or Patreon allow authors to generate recurring income through exclusive content.
- **Educational & Licensing Deals** – Partnering with schools, corporations, or training programs to license book content can open new revenue streams.
- **Audiobook & Print Expansions** – Utilizing platforms like Findaway Voices and IngramSpark expands accessibility and profitability.
- **Crowdfunding & Preorders** – Using Kickstarter or Indiegogo to fund special editions or series expansions engages readers while securing upfront sales.

Building multiple revenue sources ensures that the business remains stable even if market trends change.

Leveraging Marketing & Branding for Longevity

A sustainable publishing business depends on a recognizable brand and consistent marketing efforts that extend beyond book launches.

Long-Term Marketing Approaches:

- **Develop a Reader Funnel** – Guide readers from free content (blog, lead magnet, short story) into paid offerings.
- **Branding & Visibility** – Establish a strong author brand through a well-designed website, professional visuals, and consistent messaging.
- **Email List Mastery** – Regularly engage subscribers with updates, bonus content, and exclusive offers to build reader loyalty.
- **Evergreen Advertising** – Use low-maintenance ads on

Amazon or Facebook to keep books visible without
constant manual effort.
- **Engagement on Niche Platforms** – Be active where
target readers spend time, whether that's Goodreads,
TikTok, or YouTube.

A recognizable and trusted brand creates an audience that
follows the author beyond a single book launch.

FUTURE-PROOFING AGAINST INDUSTRY CHANGES

The publishing industry evolves quickly, with changes in
technology, distribution, and reader behavior. Authors who
future-proof their business remain competitive.

Strategies to Stay Adaptable:

- **Monitor Industry Trends** – Follow resources like ALLi,
Kindlepreneur, and The Hot Sheet to stay informed on
shifts in publishing.
- **Adapt to Subscription Models** – Platforms like Kobo
Plus and Kindle Unlimited show the rise of subscription-
based book consumption.
- **Explore AI & Automation** – While AI can assist in
content creation, it should be used as a tool rather than a
replacement for original writing.
- **Experiment with New Markets** – Foreign translations,
serialized fiction, and Web3 publishing offer emerging
opportunities.
- **Stay Financially Flexible** – Avoid reliance on a single
retailer or revenue model to maintain financial stability.

By staying adaptable, authors can seize new opportunities rather
than be disrupted by change.

Long-Term Wealth & Exit Strategies

For authors looking beyond immediate income, building a publishing business that retains value over time is essential.

Sustaining Wealth & Future Growth:

- **Build an Intellectual Property Portfolio** – Books, audiobooks, scripts, and adaptations add long-term value.
- **Sell a Backlist Catalog** – Some authors sell their publishing rights to investors or traditional publishers for lump-sum payments.
- **Create Evergreen Revenue Streams** – Books that continuously sell (e.g., non-fiction guides, classic genre fiction) provide passive income.
- **Plan for Retirement & Investments** – Royalties can be reinvested into stocks, real estate, or other long-term financial vehicles.
- **Develop Licensing & Adaptation Deals** – Selling IP for film, TV, or educational purposes extends a book's lifespan.

Building wealth in publishing isn't just about sales—it's about creating assets that continue to generate income even when an author steps back.

Additional Resources & Further Reading

Essential Tools & Platforms for Business Growth

- **Business & Productivity** – QuickBooks (finance), Trello (project management), Notion (workflow organization)
- **Marketing & Sales** – Publisher Rocket, BookBub Ads, Kit (email marketing)

- **Industry News & Learning** – ALLi, The Hot Sheet, Publisher's Weekly, Kindlepreneur

Recommended Books & Courses

- *The Business of Being a Writer* by Jane Friedman
- *Write. Publish. Repeat.* by Sean Platt & Johnny B. Truant
- *How to Market a Book* by Joanna Penn
- Online courses on Reedsy, Teachable, and Udemy

SUSTAINABLE SUCCESS IS INTENTIONAL

Long-term publishing success isn't accidental—it's built through strategic decisions, financial diversification, and adaptability. Whether an author's goal is creative independence or financial freedom, the key is to establish scalable systems that make publishing sustainable for years to come.

YOUR NEXT STEPS:

- **Define a five-year publishing and financial strategy.**
- **Identify two new revenue streams to implement within the next 12 months.**
- **Commit to continuous learning and adaptation in the publishing industry.**

Publishing is a long game, and those who think beyond individual book sales will thrive in an industry that continues to evolve. By treating writing as both an art and a business, authors can achieve both financial success and creative fulfillment.

14. Conclusion – Your Publishing Journey

Reflecting on the Path Ahead

From idea to execution, this book has provided a roadmap to transform your writing into a sustainable publishing business. Whether you started as an aspiring author or an entrepreneur leveraging books as an asset, you now have the strategies to navigate self-publishing with confidence and purpose.

> *"The key to success in publishing is not the occasional breakthrough, but the consistent commitment to your craft."*

> *— Jane Friedman*

The Journey So Far

- **Mindset & Foundation:** You learned how to shift from simply writing books to thinking like a publisher—strategizing, planning, and positioning your books for success.

- **Publishing & Marketing:** You now understand the intricacies of publishing on KDP, optimizing your book's metadata, and using proven marketing techniques to build visibility and long-term sales.
- **Scaling Your Business:** Beyond launching a book, you explored ways to grow a sustainable publishing business —diversifying income, expanding into new formats, and leveraging multiple platforms.
- **Avoiding Pitfalls & Adapting to Change:** You've gained insights into common mistakes authors make and strategies to future-proof your publishing career.

WHERE DO YOU GO FROM HERE?

The journey doesn't stop at publishing your first book—or even your tenth. Sustainable success comes from continuous learning, testing new strategies, and adapting to industry trends. The most successful authors and publishers are those who refine their approach, expand into new opportunities, and consistently engage with their readers.

YOUR NEXT STEPS:

- **Take Action:** Choose one strategy from this book and apply it immediately—whether it's optimizing your book listings, refining your marketing, or setting up an additional income stream.
- **Commit to Growth:** Treat publishing as a long-term endeavor. Experiment, learn from setbacks, and continuously refine your approach.
- **Stay Connected to the Industry:** Follow industry leaders, stay updated on new publishing trends, and be willing to adapt as the landscape evolves.

FINAL WORDS: YOUR PUBLISHING FUTURE

Self-publishing isn't just about writing books—it's about **creating a body of work** that builds financial stability and creative freedom. The power to shape your career is entirely in your hands. With strategic planning, perseverance, and a willingness to evolve, you can turn your publishing journey into a thriving business.

The question is no longer *if* you can succeed in self-publishing, but *how far* you're willing to go. Your next chapter isn't just something you write—it's something you live.

Go forth, publish, and create the future you envision.

www.ingramcontent.com/pod-product-compliance
Lightning Source LLC
Chambersburg PA
CBHW070939210326
41520CB00021B/6975